PIANO / VOCAL / GUITAR

ALTERNATIVE ROCK
SHEET MUSIC COLLECTION

ISBN 978-1-4803-9623-4

7777 W. BLUEMOUND RD. P.O. BOX 13819 MILWAUKEE, WI 53213

For all works contained herein:
Unauthorized copying, arranging, adapting, recording, Internet posting, public performance,
or other distribution of the printed music in this publication is an infringement of copyright.
Infringers are liable under the law.

Visit Hal Leonard Online at
www.halleonard.com

CONTENTS

4	ANIMAL	NEON TREES
22	BITTER SWEET SYMPHONY	THE VERVE
13	BLACK	PEARL JAM
26	BLACK HOLE SUN	SOUNDGARDEN
38	BRING ME TO LIFE	EVANESCENCE
31	CHASING CARS	SNOW PATROL
50	CLOSING TIME	SEMISONIC
43	CRAZY	GNARLS BARKLEY
58	DRIVE	INCUBUS
74	GIVES YOU HELL	THE ALL-AMERICAN REJECTS
82	GOOD RIDDANCE (TIME OF YOUR LIFE)	GREEN DAY
86	HOW YOU REMIND ME	NICKELBACK
67	I WILL FOLLOW YOU INTO THE DARK	DEATH CAB FOR CUTIE
94	IN THE END	LINKIN PARK
108	IRIS	GOO GOO DOLLS
101	JUMPER	THIRD EYE BLIND
127	KARMA POLICE	RADIOHEAD
118	KRYPTONITE	3 DOORS DOWN
132	LEARN TO FLY	FOO FIGHTERS
139	LIGHTNING CRASHES	LIVE

146	LONELY BOY	**THE BLACK KEYS**
150	THE MIDDLE	**JIMMY EAT WORLD**
160	MR. BRIGHTSIDE	**THE KILLERS**
166	ONE WEEK	**BARENAKED LADIES**
174	THE ONLY EXCEPTION	**PARAMORE**
155	RADIOACTIVE	**IMAGINE DRAGONS**
182	SANTERIA	**SUBLIME**
189	SAY IT AIN'T SO	**WEEZER**
201	SEX AND CANDY	**MARCY PLAYGROUND**
196	SMELLS LIKE TEEN SPIRIT	**NIRVANA**
204	THNKS FR TH MMRS	**FALL OUT BOY**
222	UNDER THE BRIDGE	**RED HOT CHILI PEPPERS**
213	UNWELL	**MATCHBOX TWENTY**
227	UPRISING	**MUSE**
234	USE SOMEBODY	**KINGS OF LEON**
242	WE ARE YOUNG	**FUN. FEATURING JANELLE MONÁE**
268	WHERE IS MY MIND?	**PIXIES**
248	WHERE IT'S AT	**BECK**
256	WITH ARMS WIDE OPEN	**CREED**
264	ZOMBIE	**THE CRANBERRIES**

12

B♭maj7 | **F** | **Csus2**

Oh, oh. Say good-bye to my heart to-night.

F6 | **F/A** | **Am**

Oh, oh, I want some more. Oh, oh,

Dm/A | **B♭maj7**

what are you wait-ing for? What are you wait-ing

Csus | **C** | **Csus2** | **F6**

for? Say good-bye to my heart to-night

BLACK

Music by STONE GOSSARD
Lyric by EDDIE VEDDER

BITTER SWEET SYMPHONY

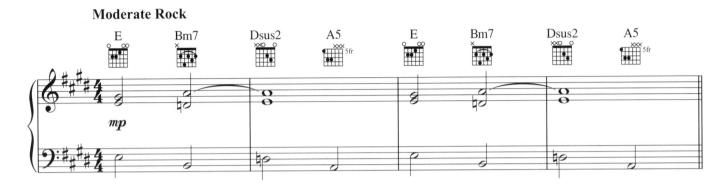

Written by MICK JAGGER and KEITH RICHARDS
Lyrics by RICHARD ASHCROFT

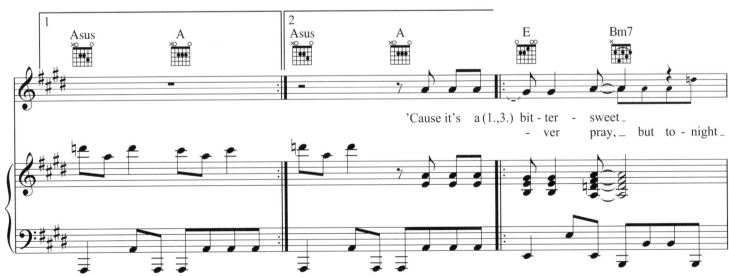

'Cause it's a (1.,3.) bit - ter - sweet_
- ver pray,_ but to - night_

© 1997 ABKCO MUSIC, INC., 85 Fifth Avenue, New York, NY 10003
All Rights Reserved   Used by Permission

BLACK HOLE SUN

Words and Music by
CHRIS CORNELL

CHASING CARS

Words and Music by GARY LIGHTBODY,
TOM SIMPSON, PAUL WILSON,
JONATHAN QUINN and NATHAN CONNOLLY

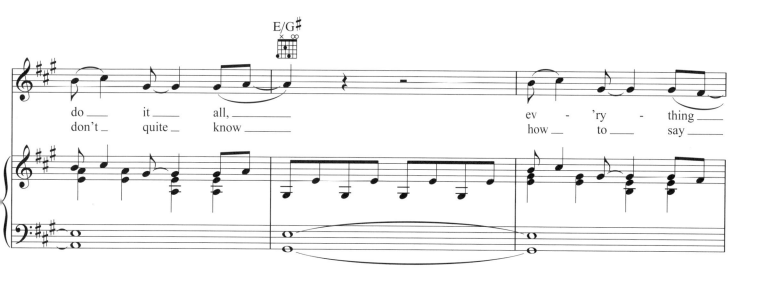

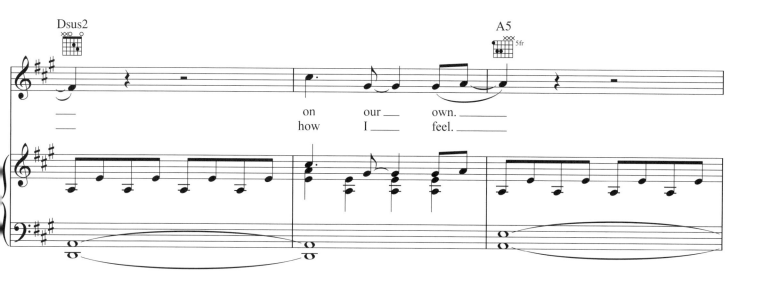

Copyright © 2006 UNIVERSAL MUSIC PUBLISHING BL LTD.
All Rights in the U.S. and Canada Controlled and Administered by UNIVERSAL - SONGS OF POLYGRAM INTERNATIONAL, INC.
All Rights Reserved   Used by Permission

BRING ME TO LIFE

Words and Music by BEN MOODY, AMY LEE and DAVID HODGES

© 2002 RESERVOIR MEDIA MANAGEMENT, INC., ZOMBIES ATE MY PUBLISHING and FORTHEFALLEN PUBLISHING
All Rights Administered by RESERVOIR MEDIA MANAGEMENT, INC.
RESERVOIR MEDIA MUSIC Administered by ALFRED MUSIC
All Rights Reserved   Used by Permission

CRAZY

43

Words and Music by BRIAN BURTON,
THOMAS CALLAWAY, GIANPIERO REVERBERI
and GIANFRANCO REVERBERI

Moderate R&B

I re-mem-ber when, I re-mem-ber, I re-mem-ber when I lost my mind.

There was some-thing so pleas-ant a-bout that place.

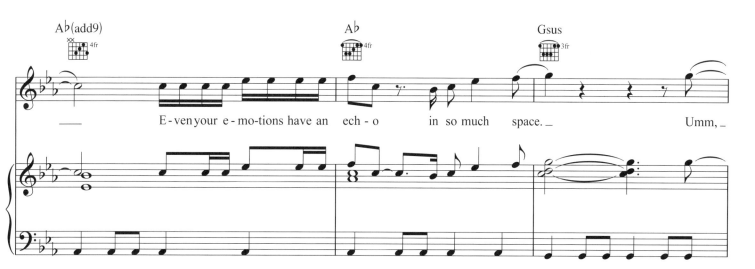

E-ven your e-mo-tions have an ech-o in so much space. Umm,

Copyright © 2006 Chrysalis Music Ltd., Warner/Chappell Music Publishing Ltd. and Universal Music Publishing Ricordi Srl
All Rights for Chrysalis Music Ltd. Administered by Chrysalis Music Group Inc., a BMG Chrysalis company
All Rights for Warner/Chappell Music Publishing Ltd. in the U.S. and Canada Administered by Warner-Tamerlane Publishing Corp.
All Rights for Universal Music Publishing Ricordi Srl in the U.S. and Canada Administered by Killer Tracks
All Rights Reserved   Used by Permission
- contains a sample of "Last Men Standing" by GianPiero Reverberi and GianFranco Reverberi

CLOSING TIME

Words and Music by
DAN WILSON

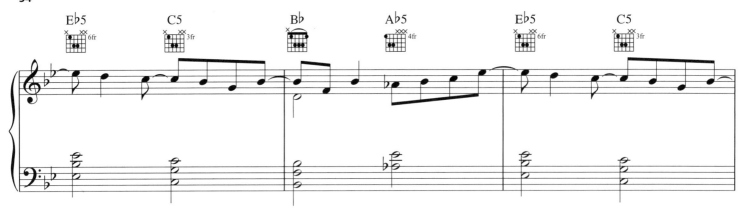
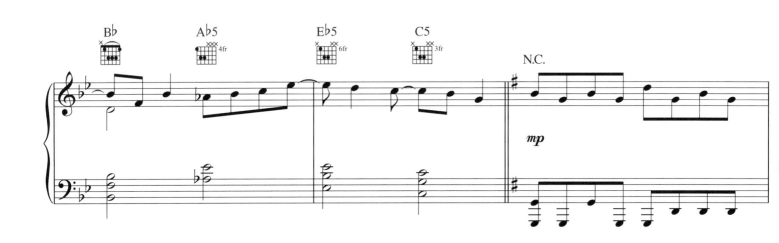

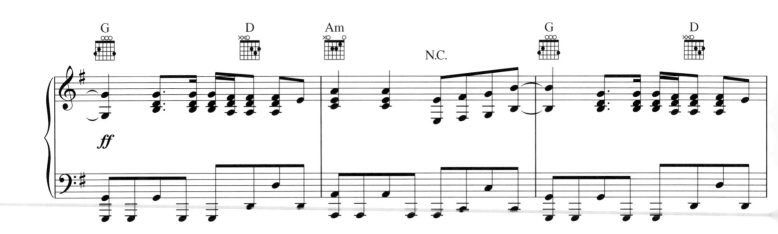

DRIVE

Words and Music by BRANDON BOYD,
MICHAEL EINZIGER, ALEX KATUNICH,
JOSE PASILLAS II and CHRIS KILMORE

© 1999 EMI APRIL MUSIC INC. and HUNGLIKEYORA MUSIC
All Rights Controlled and Administered by EMI APRIL MUSIC INC.
All Rights Reserved   International Copyright Secured   Used by Permission

I WILL FOLLOW YOU INTO THE DARK

Words and Music by
BENJAMIN GIBBARD

GOOD RIDDANCE
(Time of Your Life)

Words by BILLIE JOE
Music by GREEN DAY

IN THE END

Words and Music by ROB BOURDON,
BRAD DELSON, JOE HAHN,
MIKE SHINODA and CHARLES BENNINGTON

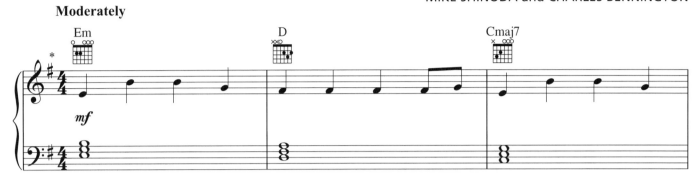

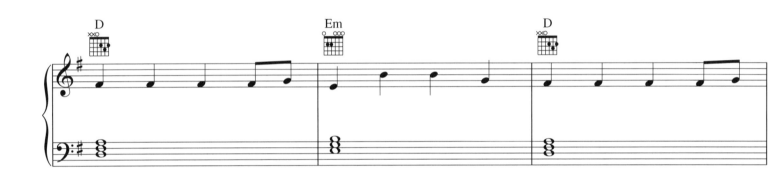

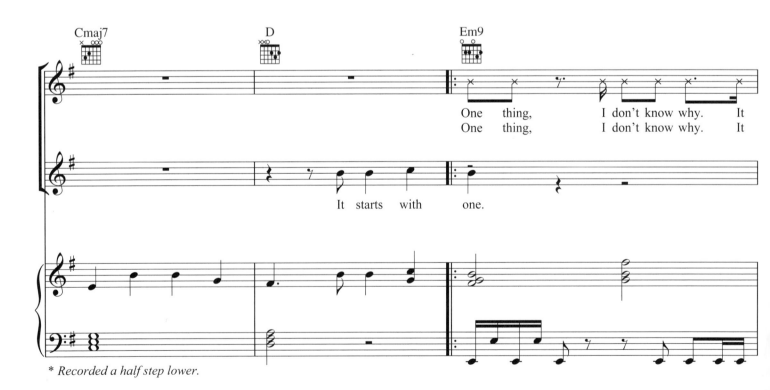

*Recorded a half step lower.

Copyright © 2000 by Universal Music - Z Songs, Rob Bourdon Music, Nondisclosure Agreement Music,
Big Bad Mr. Hahn Music, Kenji Kobayashi Music and Universal Music - Z Tunes LLC
All Rights for Rob Bourdon Music, Nondisclosure Agreement Music, Big Bad Mr. Hahn Music
and Kenji Kobayashi Music in the U.S. and Canada Administered by Universal Music - Z Songs
International Copyright Secured   All Rights Reserved

JUMPER

Words and Music by
STEPHAN JENKINS

Moderately, in 2

I wish you would step back from that ledge, my friend.

You could cut ties with all the lies that you've been living in.

And if you do not want to see me again,

Copyright © 1997 Music Of EverPop (BMI)
All Rights Administered by BMG Rights Management (US) LLC
International Copyright Secured   All Rights Reserved

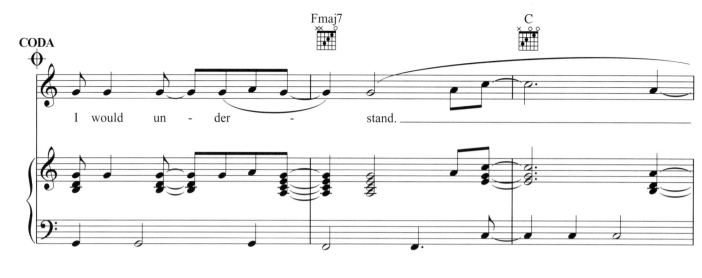

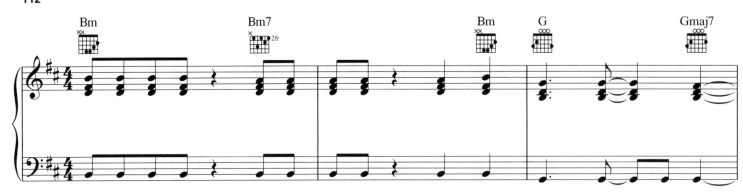
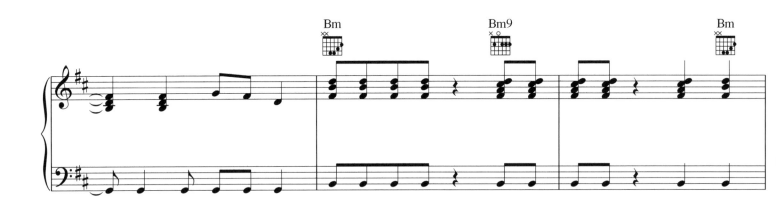

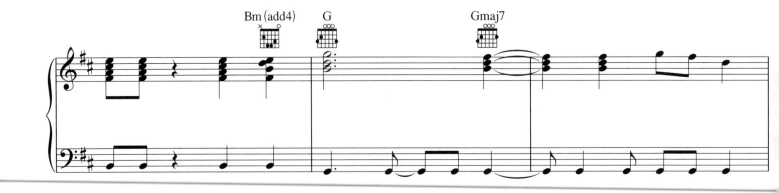

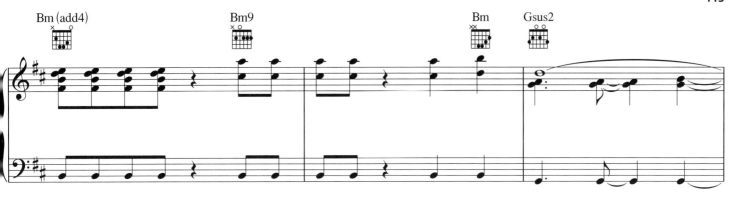

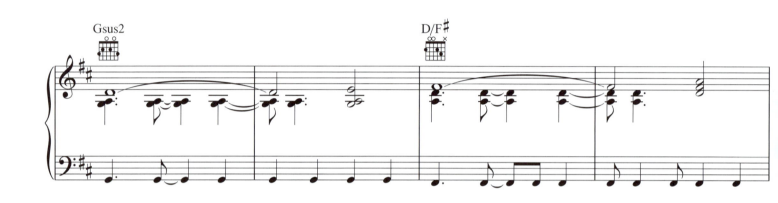

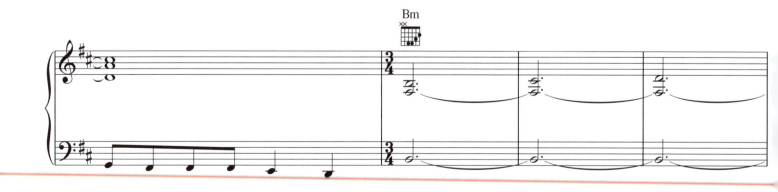

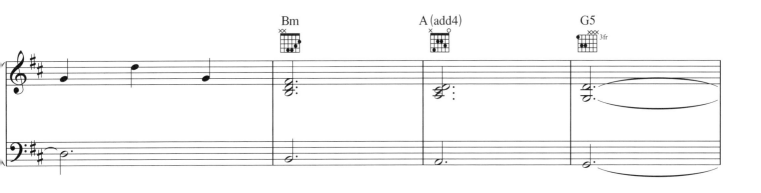

And I ____ don't want the world ____ to see ____ me

KRYPTONITE

Words and Music by MATT ROBERTS,
BRAD ARNOLD and TODD HARRELL

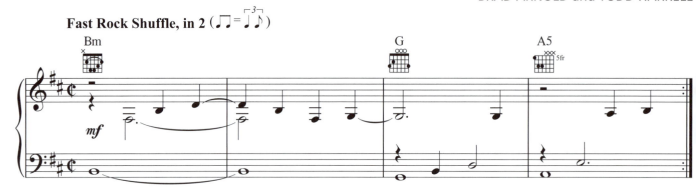

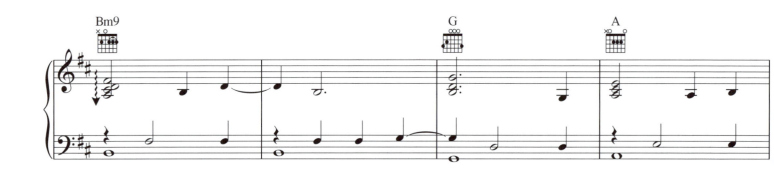

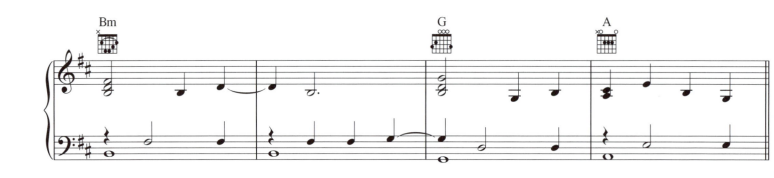

I took a walk a-round the world to ease my
I watched the world float to the dark side of the
You called me strong, you called me weak, but still your

Copyright © 2000 SONGS OF UNIVERSAL, INC. and ESCATAWPA SONGS
All Rights Controlled and Administered by SONGS OF UNIVERSAL, INC.
All Rights Reserved   Used by Permission

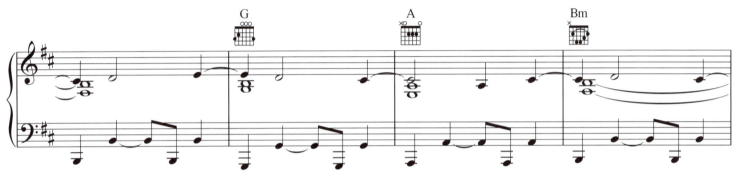
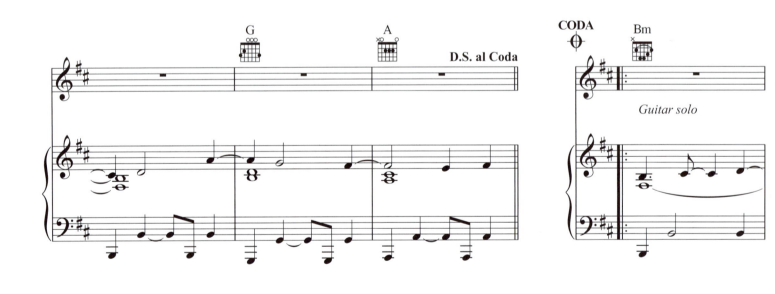
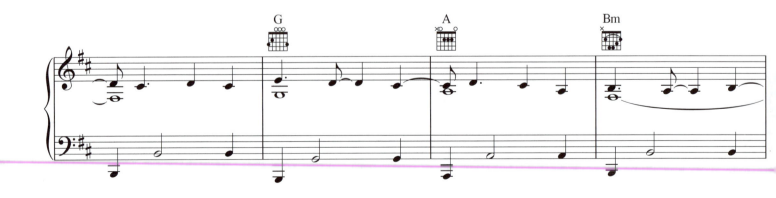

KARMA POLICE

*Words and Music by THOMAS YORKE,
JONATHAN GREENWOOD, COLIN GREENWOOD,
EDWARD O'BRIEN and PHILIP SELWAY*

© 1997 WARNER/CHAPPELL MUSIC LTD.
All Rights in the U.S. and Canada Administered by WB MUSIC CORP.
All Rights Reserved   Used by Permission

LEARN TO FLY

Words and Music by TAYLOR HAWKINS,
NATE MENDEL and DAVE GROHL

* Recorded a half step higher.

Copyright © 1999 LIVING UNDER A ROCK MUSIC, FLYING EARFORM MUSIC and M.J. TWELVE MUSIC
All Rights for LIVING UNDER A ROCK MUSIC Controlled and Administered by UNIVERSAL MUSIC CORP.
All Rights for FLYING EARFORM MUSIC Administered by KOBALT MUSIC PUBLISHING AMERICA, INC.
All Rights for M.J. TWELVE MUSIC Controlled and Administered by WARNER-TAMERLANE PUBLISHING CORP.
All Rights Reserved   Used by Permission

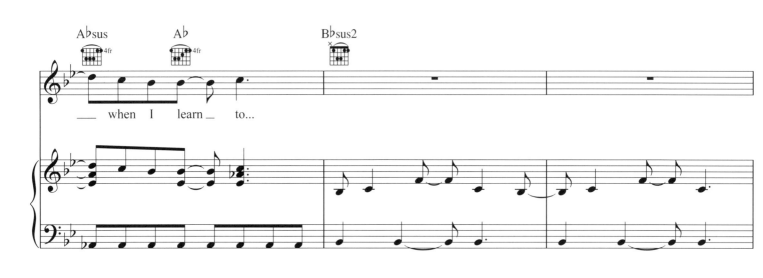

LIGHTNING CRASHES

Words and Music by EDWARD KOWALCZYK, CHAD TAYLOR, PATRICK DAHLHEIMER and CHAD GRACEY

* Recorded a half step lower.

Copyright © 1994 by Universal Music Publishing MGB Ltd.
All Rights in the U.S. Administered by Universal Music - Careers
International Copyright Secured   All Rights Reserved

LONELY BOY

Words and Music by DAN AUERBACH,
PATRICK CARNEY and BRIAN BURTON

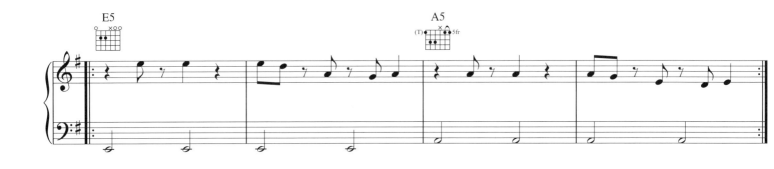

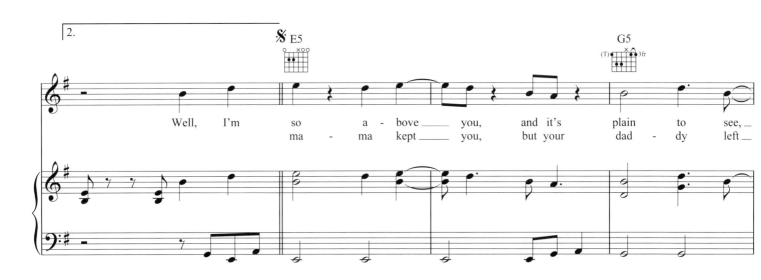

Well, I'm so a-bove you, and it's plain to see,
ma-ma kept you, but your dad-dy left

Copyright © 2011 McMoore McLesst Publishing (BMI) and Sweet Science (ASCAP)
All Rights on behalf of McMoore McLesst Publishing in the world excluding Australia and New Zealand Administered by Wixen Music Publishing, Inc.
All Rights on behalf of McMoore McLesst Publishing in Australia and New Zealand Administered by GaGa Music
All Rights Reserved   Used by Permission

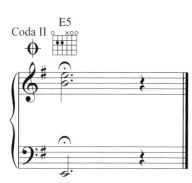

THE MIDDLE

Words and Music by JAMES ADKINS,
RICHARD BURCH, THOMAS LINTON
and ZACHARY LIND

© 2001 TURKEY ON RYE MUSIC
All Rights Administered by WB MUSIC CORP.
All Rights Reserved   Used by Permission

MR. BRIGHTSIDE

Words and Music by BRANDON FLOWERS,
DAVE KEUNING, MARK STOERMER
and RONNIE VANNUCCI

*Recorded a half step lower.

Copyright © 2004 UNIVERSAL MUSIC PUBLISHING LTD.
All Rights in the United States and Canada Controlled and Administered by UNIVERSAL - POLYGRAM INTERNATIONAL PUBLISHING, INC.
All Rights Reserved   Used by Permission

ONE WEEK

Words and Music by
ED ROBERTSON

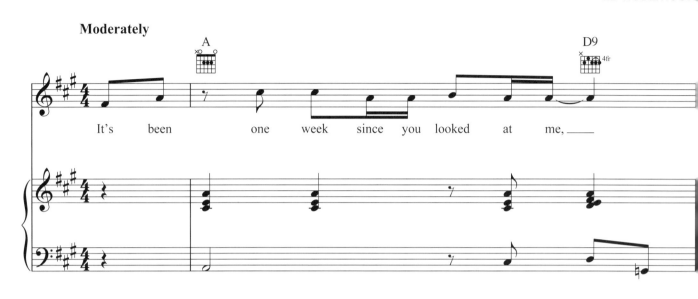

© 1998 WB MUSIC CORP. and TREAT BAKER MUSIC
All Rights Administered by WB MUSIC CORP.
All Rights Reserved Used by Permission

Additional Lyrics

2. Chickity China the Chinese chicken,
   Have a drumstick and your brain stops tickin'.
   Watchin' "X-Files" with no lights on.
   We're *dans la maison*.
   I hope the Smoking Man's in this one.
   Like Harrison Ford, I'm getting frantic.
   Like Sting, I'm tantric.
   Like Snickers, guaranteed to satisfy.
   Like Kurasawa, I make mad films.
   OK, I don't make films,
   But if I did, they'd have a Samurai.
   Gonna get a set a'better clubs;
   Gonna find the kind with tiny nubs
   Just so my irons aren't always flying
   Off the backswing.
   Gotta get in tune with Sailor Moon,
   'Cause the cartoon has got
   The boom Anime babes
   That make me think the wrong thing.
   To Bridge

THE ONLY EXCEPTION

Words and Music by HAYLEY WILLIAMS
and JOSH FARRO

* Recorded a half step lower.

© 2009 WB MUSIC CORP., BUT FATHER, I JUST WANT TO SING MUSIC, FBR MUSIC and JOSH'S MUSIC
All Rights Administered by WB MUSIC CORP.
All Rights Reserved   Used by Permission

SAY IT AIN'T SO

Words and Music by
RIVERS CUOMO

SEX AND CANDY

Words and Music by
JOHN WOZNIAK

Mellow Rock

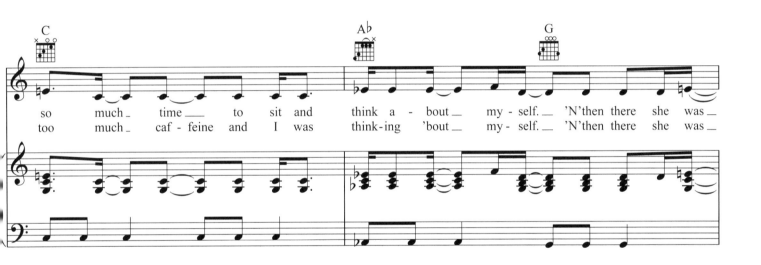

* Recorded a half step lower.

© 1997 WB MUSIC CORP. and Wozniak Publishing
All Rights Administered by WB MUSIC CORP.
All Rights Reserved   Used by Permission

THNKS FR TH MMRS

Words and Music by PATRICK STUMP,
PETER WENTZ, ANDREW HURLEY
and JOSEPH TROHMAN

I'm gon-na make you bend and break.

Say a prayer but let the good times roll in case

* Recorded a half step lower.

Copyright © 2007 Sony/ATV Music Publishing LLC and Chicago X Softcore Songs
All Rights Administered by Sony/ATV Music Publishing LLC, 424 Church Street, Suite 1200, Nashville, TN 37219
International Copyright Secured All Rights Reserved

UNWELL

Words and Music by
ROB THOMAS

Moderately slow Rock

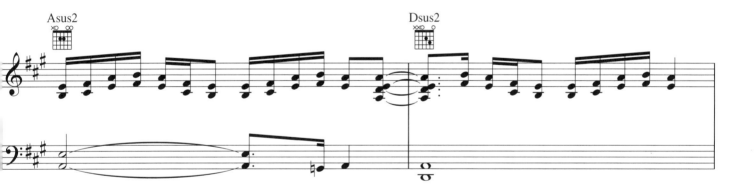

© 2002 EMI Blackwood Music Inc. and BIDNIS, INC.
All Rights Controlled and Administered by EMI BLACKWOOD MUSIC INC.
All Rights Reserved International Copyright Secured Used by Permission

216

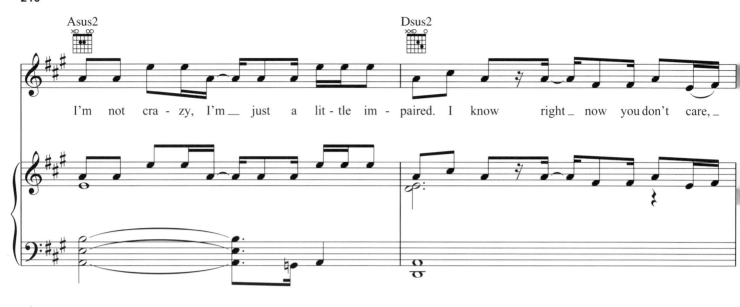

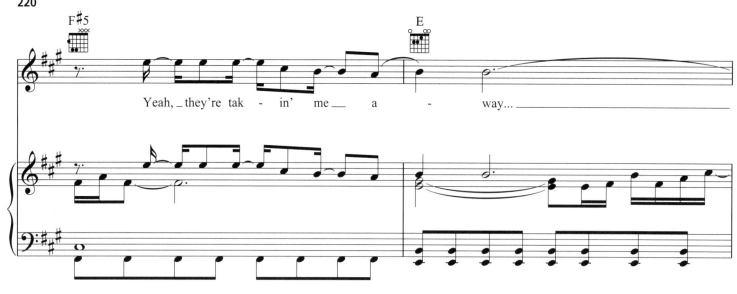
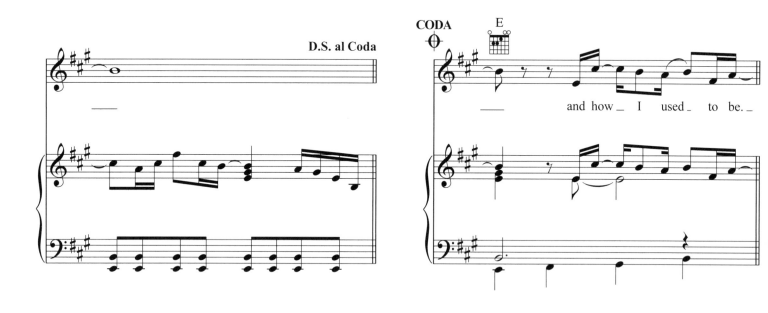
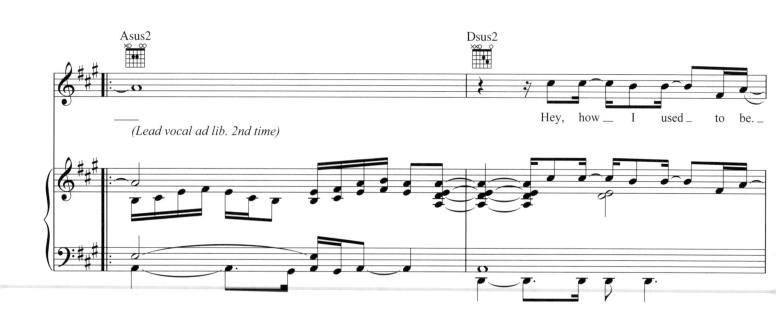

| G6 | Fmaj7 | A | Am7 |

is where I drew some blood. Under the bridge downtown

| G6 | Fmaj7 | A | Am7 |

I could not get e - nough. Under the bridge downtown

| G6 | Fmaj7 | A | Am7 |

for - got a - bout my love. Under the bridge downtown

| G6 | Fmaj7 | A | Am | G6 | Fmaj7 | A |

Play 8 times

I gave my life a - way. *Vocal ad lib.*

last time - rit.

UPRISING

Words and Music by
MATTHEW BELLAMY

USE SOMEBODY

Words and Music by CALEB FOLLOWILL,
NATHAN FOLLOWILL, JARED FOLLOWILL
and MATTHEW FOLLOWILL

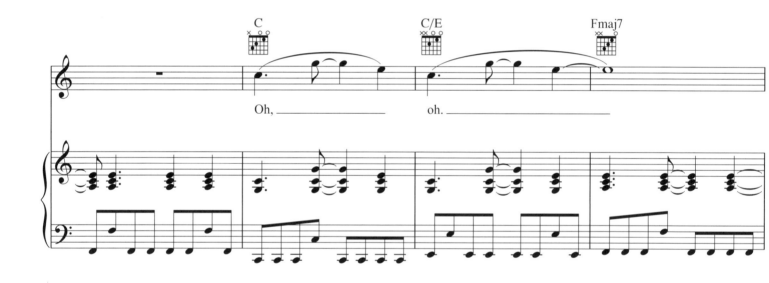
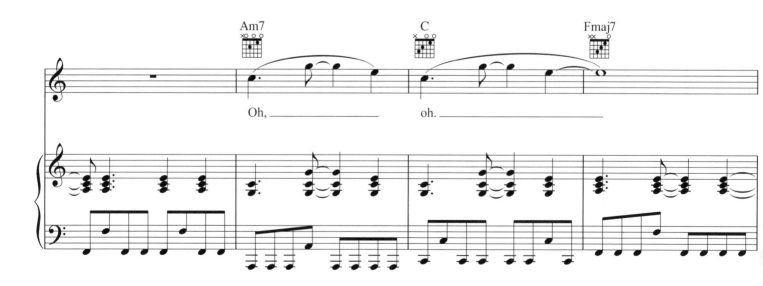

Copyright © 2008 Music Of Windswept (ASCAP), Martha Street Music (ASCAP), Followill Music (ASCAP),
McFearless Music (BMI), Coffee Tea Or Me Publishing (BMI) and Songs Of Southside Independent Publishing
All Rights for Music Of Windswept, Martha Street Music, Followill Music, McFearless Music and Coffee Tea Or Me Publishing Administered by BUG Music, Inc., a BMG Chrysalis company
International Copyright Secured All Rights Reserved

238

WE ARE YOUNG

Words and Music by JEFF BHASKER,
ANDREW DOST, JACK ANTONOFF
and NATE RUESS

Copyright © 2011, 2012 Sony/ATV Music Publishing LLC, Way Above Music, Rough Art, Shira Lee Lawrence Rick Music, WB Music Corp., FBR Music and Bearvon Music
All Rights on behalf of Sony/ATV Music Publishing LLC, Way Above Music, Rough Art and Shira Lee Lawrence Rick Music Administered by
Sony/ATV Music Publishing LLC, 424 Church Street, Suite 1200, Nashville, TN 37219
All Rights on behalf of FBR Music and Bearvon Music Administered by WB Music Corp.
International Copyright Secured   All Rights Reserved

WHERE IT'S AT

Words by BECK HANSEN
Music by BECK HANSEN, MIKE SIMPSON and JOHN KING

250

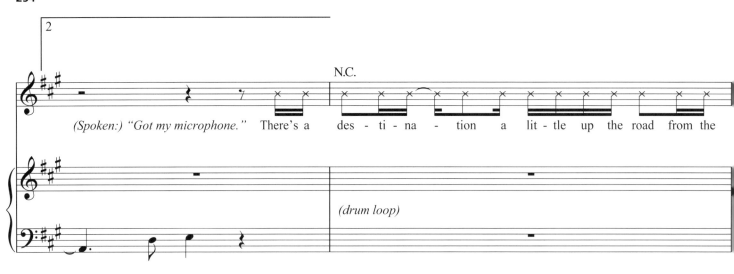
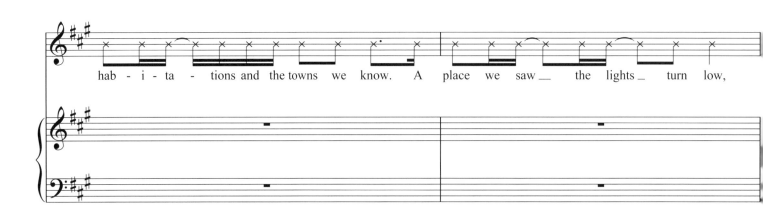
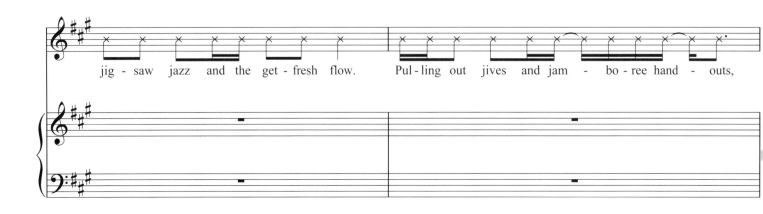
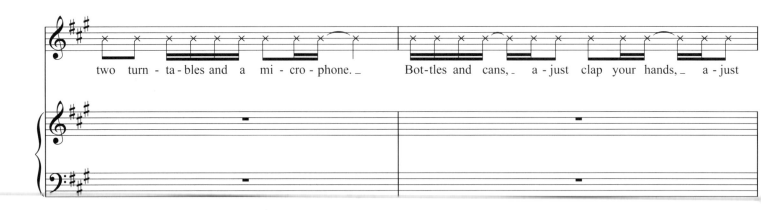

ZOMBIE

Lyrics and Music by
DOLORES O'RIORDAN

WHERE IS MY MIND?

Words and Music by
FRANK BLACK

Copyright © 1988 RICE AND BEANS MUSIC
All Rights Controlled and Administered by SONGS OF UNIVERSAL, INC.
All Rights Reserved   Used by Permission

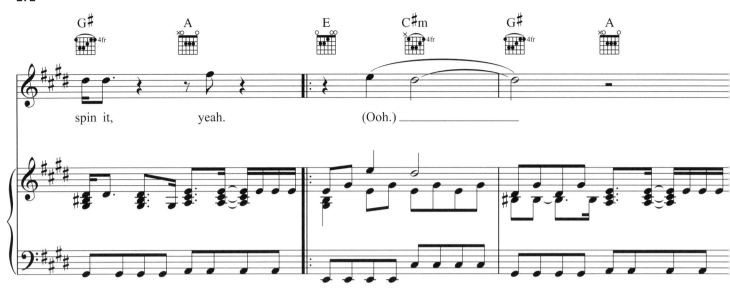
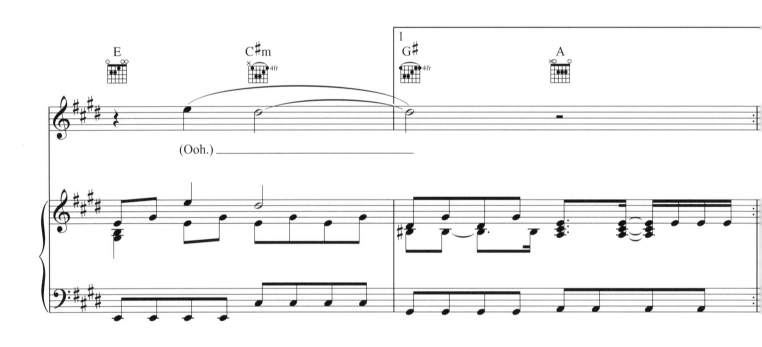
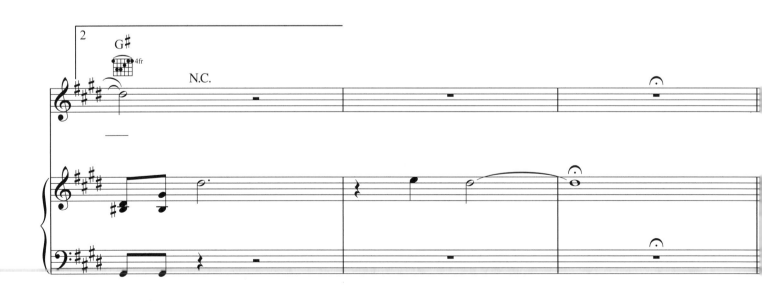